THE SUCCESSFUL SIDE HUSTLE

How to Make Money Outside of Your Day Job

JOY DANIELS

Copyright © 2024 by JOY DANIELS

TABLE OF CONTENT

INTRODUCTION

Welcome to "The Successful Side Hustle: How to Make Money Outside of Your Day Job," your comprehensive guide to unlocking financial potential beyond the confines of your 9-to-5 routine. In the dynamic landscape of today's economy, the traditional career path is no longer the sole avenue to financial success. This book is your roadmap to navigating the world of side hustles, offering practical insights, strategies, and inspiration to transform your passion into a lucrative income stream.

In a world where flexibility and adaptability are prized, cultivating a successful side hustle has become a strategic imperative. Whether you're looking to supplement your income, pursue a passion project, or transition to full-time entrepreneurship, this book provides the tools to turn your aspirations into reality. Drawing on real-life success stories, proven techniques, and a wealth of research, I've crafted a guide that caters to both the novice and the experienced side hustler.

The Successful Side Hustle isn't just about making money; it's about fostering a mindset that propels you towards financial independence. From identifying the right side hustle for your skills and interests to mastering time management and marketing, this book covers every facet of the side hustle journey. I delve into the nuances of building an online presence, leveraging social media, and optimizing productivity, ensuring you're equipped with the knowledge to thrive in the gig economy.

Join me on a transformative journey that transcends the confines of the traditional work paradigm. Whether you're a seasoned professional or just starting, "The Successful Side Hustle" is your companion to unlocking the doors of financial freedom and fulfilment. It's time to embrace the world of possibilities that await you beyond the constraints of your day job.

CHAPTER 1: THE SIDE HUSTLE LANDSCAPE

Welcome to the exploration of "The Side Hustle Landscape," the opening chapter in our journey towards mastering the art of making money outside the conventional confines of a 9-to-5 job. In this chapter, we embark on a comprehensive examination of the ever-evolving economic terrain, recognizing the seismic shifts that have paved the way for the rise of side hustles as a crucial component of financial success.

The modern work landscape is undergoing a profound transformation, with individuals seeking diverse avenues to supplement their income, pursue personal passions, and gain a greater sense of autonomy. "The Side Hustle Landscape" provides a panoramic view of this dynamic terrain, offering insights into the forces driving this shift and the myriad opportunities that arise as a result.

We begin by dissecting the fundamental changes in the global economy, unveiling the trends that have redefined traditional career paths and paved the way for the gig economy to thrive. From the rise of remote work to the increased emphasis on skills-based hiring, we delve into the factors that make the contemporary job market ripe for embracing side hustles.

Within this chapter, we also navigate the multifaceted nature of side hustles, acknowledging that they come in various shapes and sizes. Whether it's freelancing, consulting, online businesses, or passion projects turned profitable, "The Side Hustle Landscape" serves as a guide to understanding the breadth of possibilities available to ambitious individuals seeking financial independence.

As we embark on this exploration, prepare to gain a deep understanding of the economic forces at play, the societal shifts influencing work patterns, and the diverse range of opportunities that constitute the modern side hustle landscape. This chapter lays the foundation for a transformative journey, providing the context necessary to navigate the exciting world of side hustles with confidence and purpose.

- The Evolving Economy

In the 21st century, the global economy is undergoing a transformative evolution, marked by significant shifts in traditional work structures. This chapter delves into the intricate tapestry of the evolving economy, dissecting the forces that have redefined the nature of work and paved the way for the prominence of side hustles.

1. Rise of the Gig Economy

The gig economy, characterized by short-term, flexible employment, has emerged as a defining feature of the evolving economic landscape. Enabled by technological advancements, platforms connecting freelancers with employers have proliferated, giving rise to a vast ecosystem of independent workers. This section explores how the gig economy has empowered individuals to take control of their careers, providing opportunities for diversified income streams and flexible work arrangements.

2. Remote Work Revolution

Advancements in communication technology have shattered the traditional boundaries of the workplace. The rise of remote work has become a cornerstone of the evolving economy, allowing professionals to contribute to global projects without geographical constraints. This part of the chapter investigates the impact of remote work on traditional employment structures, emphasizing its role in fostering the growth of side hustles by liberating individuals from the constraints of a fixed location.

3. Skills-Based Hiring and Entrepreneurial Mindset

Employers are increasingly prioritizing skills over formal credentials, giving rise to an era of skills-based hiring. This shift is explored in depth, emphasizing how individuals with diverse talents can leverage their skill sets to create lucrative side hustles. Moreover, the chapter delves into the growing importance of cultivating an entrepreneurial mindset, essential for thriving in an economy that values innovation, adaptability, and self-directed ventures.

4. Digital Transformation

The digital revolution has permeated every aspect of modern life, including the way business is conducted. This section examines how technological advancements and the rise of online platforms have democratized entrepreneurship, providing accessible avenues for individuals to launch and promote their side hustles. From e-commerce to digital marketing, digital transformation is a driving force behind the proliferation of diverse side hustle opportunities.

5. Impact of Economic Uncertainty

The evolving economy is not without challenges. Economic uncertainties, market fluctuations, and job insecurities underscore the importance of diversifying income sources. This part of the chapter delves into how side hustles act as a financial safety net, allowing individuals to navigate the uncertainties of the job market and economic downturns with resilience.

In essence, "The Evolving Economy" is a critical lens through which we examine the seismic shifts in the world of work. Understanding these shifts is pivotal for anyone seeking to harness the full potential of side hustles in a landscape defined by flexibility, skill versatility, and the ever-present call for entrepreneurial spirit.

- Recognizing the Importance of Side Hustles

Recognizing the importance of side hustles involves a paradigm shift in understanding work, income, and personal development. This section explores the multifaceted reasons why side hustles are not just an option but a crucial strategy for financial empowerment and fulfilment.

1. Diversification of Income Streams:

One of the primary reasons for recognizing the importance of side hustles is the need for income diversification. Relying solely on a traditional 9-to-5 job may expose individuals to financial vulnerabilities. Side hustles act as supplementary income streams, providing a safety net in times of economic uncertainty and job market fluctuations.

2. Empowerment and Autonomy:

Side hustles empower individuals by offering a sense of autonomy and control over their financial destinies. Rather than being solely dependent on a single employer, individuals can leverage their skills and passions to create independent income streams. This autonomy fosters a greater sense of fulfilment and purpose in one's professional life.

3. **Passion Pursuit and Skill Development:**

Recognizing the importance of side hustles involves understanding that these ventures can be passion pursuits. Side hustles offer a platform for individuals to monetize their hobbies, interests, and talents. Moreover, they serve as a means for continuous skill development, allowing individuals to explore and enhance their capabilities beyond the confines of their primary job.

4. **Risk Mitigation and Career Flexibility:**

In a rapidly changing economic landscape, job security is no longer guaranteed. Recognizing the importance of side hustles stems from the realization that these ventures act as a form of risk mitigation. Side hustles provide individuals with a safety net, allowing them to navigate career transitions, unexpected job losses, or industry shifts with greater resilience.

5. **Wealth Building and Financial Independence:**

Side hustles are instrumental in wealth-building strategies. By generating additional income, individuals can accelerate their savings, investments, and debt repayment. This chapter explores how side hustles contribute to the journey toward financial independence, offering the potential for increased savings, investments, and long-term financial security.

6. Professional Growth and Networking:

Side hustles are not only about financial gains; they also contribute to professional growth. Recognizing their importance involves understanding how side hustles can open doors to new opportunities, expand professional networks, and enhance one's skill set. These ventures often provide a platform for personal branding and career advancement.

7. Adaptability in the Modern Workforce:

The modern workforce demands adaptability. Recognizing the importance of side hustles means acknowledging their role in adapting to the changing dynamics of work. Side hustles foster an entrepreneurial mindset, equipping individuals with the adaptability and resilience needed to thrive in an ever-evolving professional landscape.

In essence, recognizing the importance of side hustles is a pivotal step toward embracing a holistic approach to work and income. It involves a shift in mindset, from viewing side hustles as mere supplementary endeavors to recognizing them as integral components of a diversified, empowered, and fulfilling professional life.

- Navigating Challenges and Pitfalls

Embarking on the side hustle journey is a thrilling endeavor, but it's not without its challenges and pitfalls. This section comprehensively explores the nuanced process of navigating the hurdles that may arise, offering practical strategies to ensure resilience and success.

1. Identifying Common Challenges:

The first step in navigating challenges involves a clear understanding of the common obstacles encountered in the side hustle landscape. These challenges may include time constraints, competition, financial uncertainties, and the need for effective self-promotion. By identifying these hurdles, individuals can proactively prepare for and address potential roadblocks.

2. Time Management and Work-Life Balance:

Time is a precious commodity, and balancing a side hustle with a full-time job and personal life can be demanding. This section delves into effective time management strategies, emphasizing the importance of prioritization, setting realistic goals, and establishing boundaries to maintain a healthy work-life balance.

3. Financial Considerations and Investment:

Financial challenges often arise in the form of initial investment requirements, cash flow management, and unpredictable income. Navigating these pitfalls involves prudent financial planning, budgeting, and exploring creative funding options. This chapter provides insights into managing finances to sustain and grow a side hustle without compromising personal financial stability.

4. Overcoming Self-Doubt and Imposter Syndrome:

Many individuals face internal challenges such as self-doubt and imposter syndrome. Navigating these psychological pitfalls requires a focus on self-confidence, acknowledging achievements, and seeking support from mentors or communities. The chapter explores strategies to cultivate a positive mindset and overcome the mental barriers that can hinder side hustle success.

5. Legal and Regulatory Compliance:

Legal challenges, including regulatory compliance and intellectual property issues, can pose significant obstacles. Navigating these pitfalls involves gaining a basic understanding of relevant laws, trademarks, and licenses. The chapter guides legal considerations, helping side hustlers navigate the complex regulatory landscape and avoid potential legal pitfalls.

6. Effective Marketing and Branding:

Side hustles often struggle due to inadequate visibility and ineffective marketing. Navigating marketing challenges requires a strategic approach to branding, online presence, and audience engagement. This section explores the tools and techniques for creating a compelling brand story, leveraging social media, and implementing cost-effective marketing strategies.

7. Adapting to Market Trends and Competition:

Market dynamics and competition can evolve rapidly, presenting challenges for side hustlers. Navigating these challenges involves staying informed about market trends, continuously innovating, and differentiating oneself in a crowded marketplace. The chapter provides insights into monitoring industry trends and adapting side hustle strategies accordingly.

8. **Resilience and Perseverance:**

Perhaps the most crucial aspect of navigating challenges is building resilience. This section emphasizes the importance of perseverance in the face of setbacks, learning from failures, and staying committed to long-term goals. Resilience is a key attribute that distinguishes successful side hustlers from those who succumb to challenges.

By comprehensively addressing these challenges and pitfalls, individuals can approach their side hustle journey with confidence and strategic foresight. Navigating challenges becomes not just a reactive process but a proactive strategy for building a resilient and sustainable side hustle.

CHAPTER 2: DISCOVERING YOUR PASSION-DRIVEN SIDE HUSTLE

Welcome to the transformative journey of "Discovering Your Passion-Driven Side Hustle," a chapter designed to be your compass in navigating the exhilarating realm where passion and entrepreneurship intersect. In this chapter, we embark on a profound exploration of the very essence of side hustles — the alignment of your skills and interests with a venture that not only generates income but ignites your enthusiasm and purpose.

At the heart of every successful side hustle lies a profound connection to one's passions. This chapter is an invitation to introspection, a deep dive into the realms of self-discovery, where we unravel the layers of your interests, talents, and aspirations. Understanding that a side hustle is not merely an income generator but a vessel for personal fulfilment, we embark on a quest to unearth the unique blend of skills and passions that will drive your entrepreneurial pursuits.

Navigating the Landscape of Self-Discovery:

The journey begins by encouraging you to reflect on your passions and hobbies. What activities bring you joy? What skills do you possess that you find inherently satisfying? We delve into the process of identifying those areas of genuine interest, recognizing that a passion-driven side hustle is a sustainable source of motivation.

Turning Hobbies into Income Streams:

Passions often manifest in hobbies, and this chapter guides you on the transformative journey of turning these hobbies into viable income streams. Whether you're an artist, writer, or someone with a unique skill set, we explore practical strategies for monetizing your passions and creating a side hustle that aligns with your interests.

Aligning Purpose with Profit:

Discovering your passion-driven side hustle is not just about making money; it's about aligning your purpose with profit. This section emphasizes the importance of finding a venture that resonates with your values and contributes to a sense of fulfilment beyond financial gains. When passion and purpose converge, success becomes a natural byproduct.

Breaking Through Limiting Beliefs:

Often, individuals harbor limiting beliefs that hinder the exploration of their true passions. This chapter challenges and dispels such notions, guiding you towards embracing the belief that your passions are not only valid but also valuable assets that can fuel a thriving side hustle. It's about transcending self-imposed boundaries and realizing the untapped potential within.

Crafting Your Unique Side Hustle Narrative:

Every passion-driven side hustle has a unique story, and this chapter concludes by helping you articulate yours. We delve into the art of crafting a compelling narrative that not only communicates your value proposition to potential customers but also serves as a source of inspiration for your journey.

Embark on this chapter with an open mind and a sense of curiosity, as we navigate the exhilarating terrain of discovering your passion-driven side hustle. Your passions are the compass, and this chapter is your guide as you embark on a transformative odyssey towards creating a side hustle that aligns with who you are at your core.

- Assessing Your Skills and Interests

The journey to a passion-driven side hustle begins with a meticulous assessment of your skills and interests. This process is not merely an inventory but a strategic exploration, a nuanced examination of your unique combination of talents and passions. In this section, we comprehensively discuss the steps and considerations involved in the transformative task of assessing your skills and interests.

1. Self-Reflection and Inventory:

Start by engaging in deep self-reflection. Identify activities that genuinely captivate your interest and skills that come naturally to you. Consider past experiences, both personal and professional, and take stock of the tasks that you find energizing. This introspective phase lays the groundwork for a comprehensive understanding of your innate abilities.

2. Skills Audit:

Conduct a thorough skills audit to categorize your capabilities. Distinguish between hard skills (tangible, technical abilities) and soft skills (interpersonal, communication). Assess not only what you excel at in your current job but also the skills you've cultivated outside of formal employment, such as through hobbies, volunteering, or self-directed learning.

3. Passion Exploration:

Delve into your passions and interests with a curious mindset. Consider what activities make you lose track of time, ignite a sense of enthusiasm, or bring you profound joy. These are often indicative of your true passions. This stage involves exploring not just what you're good at, but what you love doing.

4. Feedback and External Perspectives:

Seek feedback from trusted friends, mentors, or colleagues. Sometimes, others can provide valuable insights into your strengths and areas where you shine. Their external perspectives can complement your self-assessment, offering a more holistic view of your skills and interests.

5. Identifying Transferable Skills:

Recognize the transferability of your skills across different domains. Skills gained in one area of your life or career might have relevance in an entirely different context. Identifying these transferable skills broadens the scope of potential side hustle opportunities and encourages creative thinking.

6. Gap Analysis:

Conduct a gap analysis to identify areas for improvement or skill development. This step is crucial for both honing existing skills and acquiring new ones that align with your interests. Consider short courses, workshops, or mentorship opportunities to bridge any gaps you identify.

7. Prioritizing and Ranking:

Prioritize your skills and interests based on your level of proficiency and passion. Create a ranked list to highlight the areas that resonate with you the most and where you can offer significant value. This prioritization serves as a foundation for selecting the most promising avenues for your passion-driven side hustle.

8. **Exploring Unconventional Talents:**

Don't overlook unconventional talents or skills that may not seem immediately applicable. Sometimes, the most unique and niche skills can become the cornerstone of a successful side hustle. Be open to exploring and leveraging these distinctive aspects of your abilities.

9. **Iterative Process and Continuous Improvement:**

Assessing your skills and interests is not a one-time task; it's an iterative process. As you gain experiences and insights through your side hustle journey, revisit and refine your assessments. Embrace a mindset of continuous improvement, adapting your skill set to align with the evolving landscape of your passion-driven endeavors.

In essence, the process of assessing your skills and interests is a strategic blueprint for crafting a passion-driven side hustle that resonates with your authentic self. By combining introspection, external perspectives, and a commitment to ongoing growth, you pave the way for a side hustle that not only leverages your unique skills but also aligns harmoniously with your deepest passions.

- Identifying Marketable Talents

Identifying marketable talents is a pivotal step in the journey towards a successful side hustle. This process involves recognizing not only what you're good at but also understanding how those skills can meet the demands of a broader audience. Here, we comprehensively discuss the strategic process of identifying and harnessing your marketable talents for a lucrative and fulfilling side hustle.

1. Self-Reflection and Skill Assessment:

Begin by conducting a thorough self-reflection and skill assessment. Identify the skills and talents you possess, considering both technical and soft skills. Reflect on your professional expertise, hobbies, and any unique abilities that set you apart. This self-awareness forms the foundation for identifying marketable talents.

2. **Research Market Demands:**

Investigate the current market demands and trends related to your skills and interests. Assess the needs of potential customers or clients. Understand what solutions or services are sought after and align your talents with these demands. Market research provides valuable insights into where your skills can create a niche.

3. **Validation through Feedback:**

Seek feedback from peers, mentors, or potential customers to validate the marketability of your talents. Honest opinions can reveal aspects you might not have considered and help refine your understanding of how your skills can address specific market needs.

4. **Identify Target Audience:**

Define your target audience. Understand who would benefit the most from your talents and skills. Consider the demographics, preferences, and pain points of your potential customers. Tailoring your talents to meet the specific needs of a well-defined audience enhances the marketability of your side hustle.

5. Evaluate Competition:

Assess the competitive landscape in your chosen niche. Identify other individuals or businesses offering similar services or products. Analyze their strengths and weaknesses. Differentiate your talents by offering a unique value proposition that sets you apart in the market.

6. Adaptability and Trend Awareness:

Talents that remain relevant are often those that adapt to changing trends. Stay informed about industry developments, emerging technologies, and shifting consumer preferences. Being aware of market trends allows you to position your talents ahead of the curve, making them more marketable.

7. **Skill Enhancement and Specialization:**

Enhance your skills and consider specialization to make your talents more marketable. Continuous learning and skill development not only improve your offerings but also demonstrate a commitment to excellence. Specialization allows you to target specific market segments more effectively.

8. **Create a Personal Brand:**

Develop a personal brand that highlights your talents. This involves crafting a compelling narrative around your skills, creating a professional online presence, and showcasing successful projects or experiences. A strong personal brand builds credibility and attracts potential clients or customers.

9. **Networking and Collaboration:**

Leverage networking opportunities to showcase your talents. Collaborate with others in your industry or related fields to expand your reach.

Networking can lead to partnerships, collaborations, and exposure that enhance the marketability of your talents.

10. **Pilot Projects and Prototypes:**

Test the marketability of your talents through pilot projects or prototypes. This allows you to gather real-world feedback, make necessary adjustments, and refine your offerings before fully launching your side hustle.

11. **Legal Considerations:**

Ensure that your talents align with legal and regulatory considerations. This involves understanding any licensing requirements, trademark issues, or industry-specific regulations that may impact the marketability of your side hustle.

In conclusion, identifying marketable talents is a strategic process that combines self-awareness, market research, adaptability, and effective branding. By aligning your skills with market demands and continuously refining your offerings, you pave the way for a successful side hustle that not only fulfils your passion but also meets the needs of a thriving market.

- Researching Niche Opportunities

Researching niche opportunities is a crucial step in the journey towards a successful and sustainable side hustle. This process involves identifying specific, underserved market segments where your skills, passions, and expertise can meet distinct needs. Below is a comprehensive discussion of the strategic process of researching niche opportunities for a thriving side hustle.

1. **Define Your Interests and Expertise:**

Begin by defining your interests, passions, and areas of expertise. This self-awareness is the foundation for exploring niche opportunities that align with your skills and resonate with your genuine interests. Consider what activities bring you joy and fulfilment.

2. Identify Market Gaps:

Conduct a thorough analysis to identify gaps or unmet needs in the market. This could involve studying existing products, services, or solutions and recognizing areas where improvement or innovation is needed. Market gaps represent potential niche opportunities that your side hustle can address.

3. Explore Your Network:

Leverage your professional and personal network to gather insights. Engage in conversations with colleagues, friends, mentors, and industry professionals to understand emerging trends, challenges, and potential areas of opportunity. Personal connections can provide valuable firsthand information about niche markets.

4. Competitor Analysis:

Analyze competitors within your industry or related fields. Identify their target audience, offerings, strengths, and weaknesses. This analysis helps you understand the competitive landscape and discover potential gaps or areas where you can differentiate your side hustle.

5. **Evaluate Market Trends:**

Stay abreast of industry trends and changes in consumer behavior. Monitor market reports, industry publications, and online resources to identify evolving patterns and preferences. Niche opportunities often arise in response to emerging trends, and being proactive in recognizing these shifts is key to success.

6. **Consumer Feedback and Reviews:**

Explore consumer feedback and reviews related to existing products or services. Online platforms, social media, and customer reviews can provide valuable insights into what customers appreciate and what they find lacking. This information can guide you in tailoring your side hustle to meet specific consumer preferences.

7. Demographic and Psychographic Analysis:

Conduct demographic and psychographic analyses of potential target audiences. Understand not only the demographics (age, gender, location) but also the psychographics (lifestyles, values, interests) of your target market. This detailed understanding enables you to tailor your offerings to a specific and receptive audience.

8. Keyword and SEO Research:

Utilize keyword research tools and SEO analysis to identify search trends and popular queries within your niche. This information helps you understand what potential customers are actively seeking, allowing you to align your side hustle with the actual demands of the market.

9. Evaluate Accessibility and Competition:

Consider the accessibility of your chosen niche. Assess the ease of entry and the level of competition. A balance must be struck between entering a niche with high demand and one that is not overly saturated, ensuring there is room for your unique value proposition.

10. Legal and Regulatory Considerations:

Investigate any legal or regulatory considerations specific to your chosen niche. This may include industry-specific regulations, licensing requirements, or intellectual property considerations. Compliance with legal standards is crucial for the long-term success of your side hustle.

11. Prototype and Test:

Develop prototypes or pilot projects to test the viability of your niche opportunity. This allows you to gather real-world feedback, refine your offerings, and ensure that there is a genuine market demand for your side hustle within the identified niche.

12. **Refinement and Iteration:**

Be prepared to refine and iterate your side hustle based on ongoing market feedback and evolving trends. The ability to adapt and continuously improve your offerings is essential for long-term success in niche markets.

By meticulously researching niche opportunities, you position your side hustle for success by addressing specific market needs, differentiating yourself from competitors, and aligning with your passions and expertise. This strategic approach enhances the sustainability and profitability of your venture in a targeted and specialized market segment.

- Balancing Passion and Profitability

Balancing passion and profitability is a delicate art, and achieving harmony between these two elements is essential for building a sustainable and fulfilling side hustle. This comprehensive discussion outlines the strategic process of navigating the intersection of passion and profitability, ensuring that your side hustle not only brings personal satisfaction but also financial success.

1. Define Your Passionate Pursuits:

Begin by clearly defining your passions. What activities, interests, or causes ignite a genuine sense of enthusiasm and joy within you? This self-awareness forms the foundation for aligning your side hustle with activities that resonate deeply with your core values.

2. Identify Profitable Opportunities within Your Passions:

Explore the intersection of your passions and potential profitability. Conduct market research to identify opportunities where your interests align with existing market demands. This step involves recognizing niches, services, or products that cater to both your fulfilment and the needs of a target audience.

3. Market Research and Validation:

Validate the market potential of your passion-driven ideas. Assess the demand, competition, and feasibility of turning your passions into a profitable venture. This research ensures that your side hustle is founded on a solid understanding of market dynamics and consumer behaviors.

4. Assess Your Unique Value Proposition:

Determine your unique value proposition within the chosen niche. What sets your passion-driven side hustle apart from others in the market? Clearly articulating the unique benefits you offer helps you stand out and attract customers willing to pay for your distinctive offerings.

5. Financial Planning and Goal Setting:

Establish realistic financial goals for your side hustle. Consider both short-term objectives and long-term aspirations. Develop a financial plan that outlines revenue targets, expenses, and investment requirements. This structured approach ensures that your passion-driven endeavors are financially viable.

6. **Evaluate Monetization Strategies:**

Explore various monetization strategies aligned with your passions. This could involve selling products, offering services, creating digital content, or exploring partnerships and collaborations. Assess the scalability and income potential of each strategy, tailoring your approach to maximize profitability.

7. **Create a Business Model:**

Develop a sustainable business model that integrates your passions and profitability goals. Define your revenue streams, cost structures, and key partnerships. A well-thought-out business model serves as a roadmap for achieving a balance between financial success and personal fulfilment.

8. **Time Management and Prioritization:**

Effectively manage your time and prioritize tasks to optimize both passion and profitability.

Balancing these elements requires strategic time allocation, focusing on income-generating activities without neglecting the aspects of your side hustle that bring you joy and satisfaction.

9. Customer Relationship Management:

Nurture strong relationships with your customers. Understand their needs, gather feedback, and adapt your offerings accordingly. Building a loyal customer base contributes to long-term profitability and provides intrinsic satisfaction as you witness the positive impact of your passion on others.

10. Adaptability and Innovation:

Stay adaptable and open to innovation. The business landscape is dynamic, and trends may evolve. Be ready to pivot or introduce innovative elements to keep your side hustle both relevant and profitable. This adaptability ensures the sustained success of your passion-driven venture.

11. Financial Sustainability and Resilience:

Prioritize financial sustainability and build resilience into your business model. Establish contingency plans, save for unforeseen challenges, and ensure that your passion-driven side hustle remains robust even in the face of economic fluctuations.

12. **Continuous Evaluation and Reflection:**

Regularly evaluate the performance of your side hustle against both passion and profitability metrics. Reflect on what aspects are working well and where adjustments may be needed. This ongoing evaluation process allows for refinement and optimization over time.

By meticulously navigating the delicate balance between passion and profitability, you cultivate a side hustle that not only aligns with your authentic self but also thrives as a financially rewarding venture. This holistic approach ensures that your passion remains the driving force behind your entrepreneurial journey, while also creating a sustainable foundation for long-term success.

CHAPTER 3: BUILDING A STRONG FOUNDATION

Welcome to the pivotal chapter, "Building a Strong Foundation," where we embark on the transformative journey of establishing the bedrock for your flourishing side hustle. In the landscape of entrepreneurial endeavors, a robust foundation is the anchor that sustains your passion, guides your decisions, and propels your side hustle towards sustainable success.

In this chapter, we delve into the essential elements that constitute a strong foundation for your side hustle – a foundation that goes beyond the tangible structures and extends into the strategic, financial, and operational aspects of your entrepreneurial venture. Whether you're just beginning your side hustle journey or looking to fortify your existing endeavors, the insights within this chapter provide a comprehensive guide to laying the groundwork for enduring success.

The Three Pillars of a Strong Foundation:

1. Setting Clear Goals and Objectives:

Begin by envisioning the destination of your side hustle journey. What are your overarching goals, both short-term and long-term? Setting clear, measurable objectives provides a roadmap for your efforts, guiding your decision-making and ensuring that every action contributes to the overarching success of your venture.

2. Creating a Sustainable Business Model:

A sustainable business model is the engine that drives your side hustle. This section explores the intricacies of developing a model that not only aligns with your passion but also addresses market demands. From revenue streams and cost structures to scalability and adaptability, we navigate the elements that make your side hustle financially resilient.

3. Legal and Financial Considerations:

Understanding the legal and financial landscape is paramount for building a strong foundation. This involves navigating licenses, registrations, and compliance requirements, as well as crafting a financial plan that safeguards your venture against uncertainties. We unravel the complexities of these considerations to empower you with the knowledge needed for a secure foundation.

The Building Blocks of Success:

- Establishing a Professional Online Presence:

In an increasingly digital world, your online presence is often the first impression potential customers have of your side hustle. This chapter delves into the strategies for creating a professional and compelling online identity that enhances visibility, credibility, and customer engagement.

- Crafting Your Brand Story:

Your brand story is the narrative that connects your passion with your audience. We explore the art of storytelling, guiding you in creating a brand narrative that not only communicates your values but also resonates with your target market. A compelling brand story is the cornerstone of building lasting connections with your audience.

- Strategic Networking and Collaborations:

Building a strong foundation extends beyond individual efforts. Strategic networking and collaborations amplify your reach, opening doors to valuable partnerships and opportunities. This section provides insights into effective networking strategies and navigating collaborations that contribute to the resilience of your side hustle.

As we embark on this chapter, envision your side hustle as a structure that stands the test of time. The insights and practical guidance within "Building a Strong Foundation" equip you with the tools to fortify your venture, ensuring that it not only survives but thrives in the dynamic landscape of entrepreneurship. Let's lay the groundwork for a side hustle that becomes a lasting testament to your passion, resilience, and entrepreneurial spirit.

- Setting Clear Goals and Objectives

Establishing clear goals and objectives is the foundational step toward building a successful side hustle. This comprehensive discussion explores the strategic process of defining and aligning your goals, providing a roadmap that propels your entrepreneurial venture toward sustainable success.

1. **Vision and Mission Definition:**

Begin by defining your overarching vision and mission. Your vision encapsulates the long-term impact you aspire to make, while the mission outlines the fundamental purpose of your side hustle. These foundational elements serve as guiding lights, shaping the goals that will drive your daily efforts.

2. SMART Goal Framework:

Employ the SMART criteria - Specific, Measurable, Achievable, Relevant, and Time-bound - to structure your goals. Specific goals provide clarity, measurable goals offer quantifiable benchmarks, achievable goals ensure feasibility, relevant goals align with your mission, and time-bound goals create a sense of urgency.

3. Short-Term and Long-Term Objectives:

Distinguish between short-term and long-term objectives. Short-term goals propel immediate action, providing stepping stones toward larger, long-term aspirations. Long-term objectives align with your overarching vision, creating a cohesive trajectory for sustained growth and impact.

4. Prioritization and Sequencing:

Prioritize your goals based on their significance and impact. Determine the sequence in which goals should be pursued, ensuring that each achievement builds upon the previous one. This strategic sequencing optimizes your efforts and maintains a sense of progression.

5. Alignment with Personal Values:

Ensure that your goals align with your values. A side hustle deeply rooted in your values not only fosters intrinsic motivation but also enhances the authenticity and sustainability of your entrepreneurial journey. Aligning goals with values creates a purpose-driven venture.

6. Quantitative and Qualitative Metrics:

Define both quantitative and qualitative metrics to measure goal attainment. Quantitative metrics include numerical benchmarks, while qualitative metrics capture the intangible aspects of success, such as customer satisfaction, brand reputation, or personal fulfilment.

7. Feedback and Iteration:

Foster a culture of feedback and iteration. Regularly assess your progress toward goals, seeking input from mentors, peers, or customers.

Use this feedback to refine and iterate your objectives, ensuring that they remain relevant and responsive to changing circumstances.

8. Risk Analysis and Contingency Planning:

Conduct a risk analysis to identify potential obstacles or challenges. Develop contingency plans to mitigate risks and adapt to unforeseen circumstances. This proactive approach enhances the resilience of your goals, allowing you to navigate setbacks with agility.

9. Integration with Business Model:

Integrate your goals seamlessly with your overall business model. Ensure that each goal contributes directly to the sustainability and profitability of your side hustle. Alignment with your business model enhances the strategic coherence of your objectives.

10. Communication and Transparency:

Communicate your goals to relevant stakeholders, including team members, collaborators, or investors. Transparency fosters alignment and shared commitment. It also creates a framework for accountability, encouraging collective efforts toward goal attainment.

11. **Personal Development Objectives:**

Include personal development objectives in your goal-setting process. This could involve acquiring new skills, expanding your network, or enhancing your leadership capabilities. Personal growth complements the success of your side hustle and contributes to your overall fulfilment.

12. **Celebrating Milestones:**

Celebrate milestones and achievements along the way. Recognizing progress reinforces motivation and provides an opportunity for reflection. Milestone celebrations contribute to a positive and resilient mindset, crucial for sustaining momentum in your side hustle journey.

By meticulously following this strategic blueprint for goal-setting, you establish a clear roadmap that directs your side hustle toward success. Setting clear goals and objectives not only provides focus and direction but also serves as the guiding force that transforms your passion into a purpose-driven, thriving entrepreneurial venture.

- Creating a Sustainable Business Model

Crafting a sustainable business model is the cornerstone of building a side hustle that withstands challenges, adapts to market dynamics, and thrives over the long term. This comprehensive discussion outlines the strategic process of creating a business model that integrates seamlessly with your passion and ensures the financial resilience of your entrepreneurial venture.

1. Understand Your Value Proposition:

Clearly articulate your value proposition – the unique value your side hustle offers to customers. Identify the specific problems or needs your product or service addresses and how it differentiates itself from existing solutions. A compelling value proposition forms the basis of your sustainable business model.

2. Define Revenue Streams:

Identify and diversify revenue streams that align with your offerings. This could include product sales, service fees, subscription models, licensing, or affiliate marketing. A well-defined mix of revenue streams ensures financial stability and reduces dependency on a single source.

3. Cost Structures and Operational Efficiency:

Analyze your cost structures and ensure operational efficiency. Identify fixed and variable costs, optimizing processes to maximize efficiency. This involves scrutinizing expenses, negotiating favorable terms with suppliers, and adopting technology to streamline operations.

4. Customer Segmentation and Targeting:

Clearly define your target audience through customer segmentation. Understand the demographics, behaviors, and preferences of your ideal customers. Tailor your products or services to meet their specific needs, ensuring that your business model resonates with your target market.

5. Distribution Channels:

Determine effective distribution channels to reach your customers. Whether through e-commerce platforms, partnerships, brick-and-mortar stores, or a combination of these, selecting the right channels is crucial. An optimal distribution strategy enhances accessibility and market reach.

6. Scalability and Growth Strategies:

Design your business model with scalability in mind. Evaluate growth strategies that align with your goals, such as expanding product lines, entering new markets, or leveraging technology. Scalability ensures that your side hustle can grow without compromising efficiency.

7. Customer Relationships and Retention:

Cultivate strong customer relationships to foster loyalty and repeat business. Develop strategies for customer retention, such as loyalty programs, personalized communication, or exceptional customer service. Satisfied and loyal customers contribute significantly to the sustainability of your business.

8. Adaptability to Market Trends:

Build adaptability into your business model to respond effectively to changing market trends. Stay informed about industry shifts, emerging technologies, and evolving customer preferences. An adaptable business model allows you to pivot and capitalize on new opportunities.

9. Innovation and Differentiation:

Foster a culture of innovation to continuously differentiate your offerings. Whether through product innovation, process improvements, or unique marketing strategies, staying ahead of the competition requires a commitment to ongoing creativity and differentiation.

10. Legal and Regulatory Compliance:

Ensure compliance with legal and regulatory requirements specific to your industry. Address issues such as licensing, permits, trademarks, and data protection. Compliance safeguards your business from legal challenges and reinforces its legitimacy.

11. Environmental and Social Responsibility:

Consider incorporating environmental and social responsibility into your business model. Consumers increasingly value businesses that demonstrate ethical practices. Integrating sustainability initiatives or supporting social causes can enhance your brand's reputation and appeal.

12. Financial Planning and Contingency:

Develop a robust financial plan that includes contingency measures. Anticipate potential risks and establish reserves to navigate unforeseen challenges. A well-prepared financial strategy enhances the resilience of your business model, ensuring its ability to weather economic uncertainties.

13. Continuous Monitoring and Iteration:

Implement systems for continuous monitoring and evaluation. Regularly assess key performance indicators, customer feedback, and market trends. This iterative process allows you to refine and optimize your business model over time, ensuring its relevance and effectiveness.

In summary, creating a sustainable business model is a strategic endeavor that combines a deep understanding of your value proposition, efficient operations, customer-centric approaches, and adaptability to changing market dynamics. By meticulously navigating this process, you fortify your side hustle with a foundation that not only supports its current success but also propels it toward enduring, long-term viability.

- Legal and Financial Considerations

Navigating the legal and financial landscape is critical for establishing a robust foundation for your side hustle. This comprehensive discussion explores the strategic process of addressing legal and financial considerations, ensuring compliance, minimizing risks, and fostering the financial health of your entrepreneurial venture.

Legal Considerations:

1. Business Structure:

Choose an appropriate business structure, such as a sole proprietorship, partnership, limited liability company (LLC), or corporation. Each structure has distinct legal implications regarding liability, taxes, and management. Selecting the right structure aligns with your goals and protects your assets.

2. Registration and Licensing:

Register your side hustle with the relevant
authorities and obtain any necessary licenses or
permits. Compliance with local, state, and federal
regulations is crucial. This step establishes the legal
legitimacy of your business and prevents potential
legal challenges.

3. Intellectual Property Protection:

Identify and protect your intellectual property.
This includes trademarks for your brand, copyrights
for creative works, and patents for unique
inventions or processes. Securing intellectual
property safeguards your business from
infringement and enhances its long-term value.

4. Contracts and Agreements:

Draft clear and comprehensive contracts for
business transactions, partnerships, or

collaborations. These agreements outline the rights, responsibilities, and expectations of all parties involved. Well-crafted contracts serve as legal safeguards and mitigate the risk of disputes.

5. Data Protection and Privacy:

Implement measures to ensure data protection and privacy compliance, especially if your side hustle involves handling customer or employee data. Adhering to privacy regulations enhances trust with stakeholders and protects against legal repercussions.

6. Employment Laws and Compliance:

Familiarize yourself with employment laws if your side hustle involves hiring employees or contractors. Comply with wage and hour regulations, workplace safety standards, and anti-discrimination laws. Adhering to employment laws fosters a positive work environment and mitigates legal risks.

7. Tax Obligations:

Understand your tax obligations at the local, state, and federal levels. Keep accurate financial records, track deductible expenses, and consider consulting with a tax professional to optimize your tax strategy. Complying with tax regulations is essential for financial stability and legal standing.

8. Dispute Resolution Mechanisms:

Establish mechanisms for dispute resolution, such as arbitration or mediation clauses in contracts. These alternative dispute resolution methods can be more efficient and cost-effective than traditional litigation, reducing the legal burden on your side hustle.

Financial Considerations:

1. Financial Planning and Budgeting:

Develop a comprehensive financial plan and budget for your side hustle. Project income, expenses, and cash flow to ensure financial stability. Regularly review and update your financial plan to adapt to changing circumstances and goals.

2. Emergency Fund and Reserves:

Build an emergency fund and reserves to handle unforeseen challenges or economic downturns. Maintaining financial reserves provides a safety net for your side hustle, allowing it to weather disruptions without compromising operations.

3. Credit Management:

Manage business credit responsibly. Establish a separate business bank account, monitor credit scores, and pay bills on time. Responsible credit management enhances your financial credibility and opens doors to potential financing opportunities.

4. Insurance Coverage:

Assess and secure appropriate insurance coverage for your side hustle. This may include general liability insurance, property insurance, professional liability insurance, or other industry-specific coverage. Insurance protects your business from unforeseen risks and liabilities.

5. Financial Reporting and Compliance:

Adhere to financial reporting requirements and compliance standards. Keep accurate and transparent financial records, file taxes on time, and comply with any regulatory reporting obligations. Financial transparency enhances trust with stakeholders and supports legal compliance.

6. Investment and Financing Strategies:

Explore prudent investment and financing strategies aligned with your business goals. Whether seeking external funding, managing loans, or reinvesting profits, strategic financial decisions contribute to the growth and sustainability of your side hustle.

7. Pricing Strategies and Profitability:

Develop effective pricing strategies that ensure profitability while remaining competitive in the market. Regularly review pricing models based on market trends, costs, and customer value. A balanced approach to pricing supports financial sustainability.

8. Financial Accountability and Auditing:

Implement financial accountability measures, including regular audits or reviews. Transparent financial practices foster trust among stakeholders and allow for early identification and resolution of any financial irregularities.

9. Retirement and Long-Term Planning:

Incorporate retirement and long-term financial planning into your overall strategy. Establish retirement accounts, explore investment options, and plan for the future financial health of both yourself and your business.

10. Educational and Advisory Resources:

Stay informed about financial best practices and legal updates. Utilize educational resources and consider seeking advice from financial and legal professionals. Continuous learning and professional advice contribute to informed decision-making and risk management.

By addressing these legal and financial considerations meticulously, you fortify the foundation of your side hustle. This proactive approach not only ensures compliance with legal standards but also positions your venture for long-term financial success and resilience.

- Establishing a Professional Online Presence

Building a professional online presence is essential in today's digital landscape. This comprehensive discussion explores the strategic process of establishing a digital identity that enhances visibility, credibility, and engagement for your side hustle.

1. **Define Your Brand Identity:**

Begin by clearly defining your brand identity. Identify your unique value proposition, mission, and core values. Your online presence should reflect these elements consistently across all digital platforms, creating a cohesive and recognizable brand image.

2. Choose a Domain Name:

Select a memorable and relevant domain name for your website. Ensure it aligns with your brand and is easy for users to remember. A cohesive domain name contributes to brand recognition and facilitates online search ability.

3. Build a Professional Website:

Invest in a professional and user-friendly website. Choose a clean design, intuitive navigation, and mobile responsiveness. Your website serves as the central hub for your online presence, providing a platform for showcasing products, services, and brand storytelling.

4. Optimize for Search Engines (SEO):

Implement search engine optimization (SEO) strategies to enhance your website's visibility on search engines. Conduct keyword research, optimize content, and ensure technical SEO elements are in place. Improved search rankings increase the likelihood of reaching your target audience.

5. Create Engaging Content:

Develop high-quality and engaging content that aligns with your brand. Regularly publish blog posts, articles, or multimedia content relevant to your industry. Content creation not only establishes your expertise but also encourages user interaction and boosts SEO.

6. Leverage Social Media Platforms:

Identify and prioritize social media platforms that align with your target audience. Establish profiles on platforms such as LinkedIn, Instagram, Twitter, or Facebook. Consistently share valuable content, engage with your audience, and use social media as an extension of your brand identity.

7. **Professional Photography and Visuals:**

Invest in professional photography and visuals. High-quality images convey a polished and professional image. Visual elements should align with your brand aesthetic and create a visually appealing online environment.

8. **Develop a Content Calendar:**

Create a content calendar to plan and schedule your online activities. This includes blog posts, social media updates, and any other digital content. A content calendar ensures consistency and allows for strategic planning of promotional campaigns or product launches.

9. **Implement Email Marketing:**

Build and maintain an email list to engage with your audience directly. Implement email marketing campaigns to share updates, promotions, and valuable content. Email remains a powerful tool for nurturing customer relationships and driving conversions.

10. Online Networking and Collaboration:

Actively participate in online networking. Join industry-related forums, engage in discussions on social media, and collaborate with influencers or other businesses. Networking expands your reach and can lead to valuable partnerships or collaborations.

11. Customer Reviews and Testimonials:

Encourage and showcase customer reviews and testimonials on your website and social media. Positive reviews build trust and credibility. Respond to customer feedback promptly, demonstrating a commitment to customer satisfaction.

12. Online Advertising and Promotion:

Consider online advertising strategies, such as pay-per-click (PPC) campaigns or social media ads. Targeted advertising increases your online visibility and can drive traffic to your website or specific promotions.

13. Monitor Analytics and Metrics:

Utilize analytics tools to monitor the performance of your online presence. Track website traffic, social media engagement, and email campaign metrics. Analyzing data provides insights into user behavior and helps refine your online strategy.

14. **Cybersecurity Measures:**

Implement cybersecurity measures to protect your online presence. Secure your website with SSL certificates, use strong passwords, and stay informed about potential security threats. A secure online environment safeguards your brand reputation and customer trust.

15. **Adaptability to Trends:**

Stay abreast of digital trends and technological advancements. Embrace emerging platforms, technologies, or content formats that align with your brand and resonate with your audience. Adaptability ensures that your online presence remains current and relevant.

16. **Regular Updates and Maintenance:**

Regularly update your website content, refresh visuals, and adapt your online strategy based on evolving trends. Maintenance ensures that your online presence reflects current offerings and maintains a contemporary and engaging appeal.

By following this strategic process, you not only establish a professional online presence for your side hustle but also create a dynamic and responsive digital environment. A well-crafted online identity enhances brand visibility, fosters customer trust, and positions your side hustle for success in the digital realm.

CHAPTER 4: MASTERING TIME MANAGEMENT AND PRODUCTIVITY

Welcome to the transformative chapter on "Mastering Time Management and Productivity," where we embark on a journey to unlock the full potential of your side hustle. In the dynamic realm of entrepreneurship, effective time management is the linchpin that propels passion into tangible success. This chapter delves into strategic approaches, practical techniques, and mindset shifts that empower you to navigate the demands of your side hustle with efficiency and focus.

The Essence of Time Mastery:

In the fast-paced world of side hustles, where the balance between your entrepreneurial pursuits and other life commitments can be intricate, mastering time management is a skill that differentiates the thriving from the overwhelmed. Time, once spent, is irretrievable, making its judicious utilization a cornerstone of productivity and success.

Key Themes Explored in this Chapter:

1. Prioritization and Goal Alignment:

Uncover the art of prioritization and aligning your daily tasks with the overarching goals of your side hustle. By understanding what truly matters and focusing on high-impact activities, you can navigate through the noise and channel your efforts where they yield the greatest results.

2. Effective Planning and Time Blocking:

Explore the power of effective planning and time blocking. Learn how to structure your days, weeks, and months to optimize productivity. Time blocking ensures that each facet of your side hustle receives dedicated attention, fostering a sense of control over your schedule.

3. Tools and Technologies for Efficiency:

Delve into a myriad of tools and technologies designed to enhance efficiency. From project management platforms to productivity apps, discover how leveraging technology can streamline tasks, facilitate collaboration, and amplify your overall effectiveness.

4. Mindset Shifts for Productivity:

Unearth mindset shifts that catalyze enhanced productivity. From overcoming procrastination to embracing a growth mindset, cultivating the right mental frameworks is fundamental to navigating the challenges inherent in entrepreneurship.

5. Balancing Multiple Priorities:

Learn techniques for balancing the demands of your side hustle with other life priorities. Whether juggling a day job, family commitments, or personal pursuits, effective time management strategies empower you to find equilibrium and thrive in diverse aspects of life.

6. Strategies for Overcoming Time Wasters:

Identify and overcome common time wasters that impede productivity. This section provides insights into mitigating distractions, managing interruptions, and optimizing your work environment to foster sustained focus.

7. Continuous Improvement and Adaptability:

Embrace a culture of continuous improvement and adaptability. Discover how to learn from your experiences, iterate on your processes, and stay agile in the face of evolving challenges. The ability to adapt ensures that your time management strategies remain effective over the long term.

The Ripple Effect of Time Mastery:

As you embark on this exploration of mastering time management and productivity, envision the ripple effect these skills will have on your side hustle. Beyond merely managing time, this chapter equips you with the tools to shape time to your advantage, fostering a harmonious blend of productivity, fulfilment, and success.

Prepare to unlock a new level of efficiency, focus, and achievement as we delve into the intricacies of mastering time management within the context of your unique side hustle journey. Let's embark on this transformative expedition towards unleashing the full potential of your entrepreneurial endeavors.

- Balancing Day Job and Side Hustle

Balancing a day job and a side hustle is a formidable challenge that many aspiring entrepreneurs face. This comprehensive discussion explores the strategic process of harmonizing these dual commitments, ensuring optimal performance in both spheres while maintaining personal well-being.

1. **Define Clear Goals and Priorities:**

Begin by defining clear goals for both your day job and side hustle. Understand the overarching purpose of each commitment and set realistic expectations. Prioritize tasks based on importance and align your efforts with the desired outcomes in both areas of your professional life.

2. **Effective Time Management:**

Master the art of time management. Create a detailed schedule that includes dedicated time blocks for your day job, side hustle, and personal activities. Utilize tools like calendars, planners, or productivity apps to stay organized and ensure that each aspect of your life receives the attention it deserves.

3. **Prioritize High-Impact Tasks:**

Identify high-impact tasks that contribute significantly to the success of your day job and side hustle. Focus on activities that generate the most value and align with your goals. Prioritizing these tasks allows you to make the most of your limited time and resources.

4. **Set Boundaries and Manage Expectations:**

Establish clear boundaries between your day job and your side hustle. Communicate transparently with your employer about your commitments outside of work hours. Set realistic expectations with clients, collaborators, or customers in your side hustle to manage their expectations regarding response times and availability.

5. Optimize Your Work Environment:

Create an optimized work environment for both your day job and side hustle. Minimize distractions, organize your workspace, and ensure that you have the necessary tools and resources readily available. An efficient work environment enhances your focus and productivity.

6. Utilize Breaks and Downtime:

Capitalize on breaks and downtime during your day job to attend to smaller tasks related to your side hustle. Whether responding to emails, conducting research, or brainstorming ideas, using these pockets of time efficiently contributes to the progress of your entrepreneurial venture.

7. **Delegate and Outsource:**

Recognize when it's appropriate to delegate or outsource certain tasks. Whether at your day job or side hustle, offloading non-core activities allows you to focus on responsibilities that require your specific expertise. Delegation is a valuable strategy for optimizing your time and skills.

8. **Embrace Flexibility and Adaptability:**

Embrace flexibility in your approach to balancing dual commitments. Recognize that unforeseen challenges may arise, requiring adjustments to your schedule or priorities. Cultivate adaptability to navigate these changes with resilience and maintain a healthy work-life balance.

9. **Maintain Self-Care Practices:**

Prioritize self-care to sustain your well-being. Balancing a day job and side hustle can be demanding, making self-care crucial for preventing burnout. Dedicate time for relaxation, exercise, and activities that rejuvenate your mind and body.

10. Communicate Effectively:

Foster effective communication in both your day job and side hustle. Keep your colleagues, supervisors, or team members informed about your availability, progress, and any potential challenges. Transparent communication builds trust and understanding in both professional realms.

11. Evaluate and Adjust Regularly:

Regularly evaluate the effectiveness of your balancing strategies. Assess your performance in both your day job and side hustle, and be open to making adjustments based on lessons learned. Continuous self-reflection ensures that your balancing act remains dynamic and sustainable.

12. Financial Planning and Goal Setting:

Develop a robust financial plan that accounts for income from both your day job and side hustle. Set clear financial goals for your entrepreneurial venture, considering the long-term vision and the potential for your side hustle to evolve into a full-time pursuit.

13. **Build a Support System:**

Cultivate a support system that understands and encourages your dual commitments. Whether it's friends, family, or mentors, having a support network provides emotional reinforcement and practical assistance when needed.

14. **Explore Synergies Between Roles:**

Identify synergies between your day job and your side hustle. Look for opportunities where skills or knowledge gained in one role can complement the other. Synergies enhance efficiency and create a more cohesive professional identity.

15. **Plan for Transition (If Applicable):**

If your ultimate goal is to transition from a day job to full-time entrepreneurship, plan for this transition strategically. Set milestones, assess financial readiness, and gradually increase the time and resources dedicated to your side hustle as it gains traction.

Balancing a day job and side hustle demands planning, disciplined execution, and a commitment to maintaining your overall well-being. By strategically navigating these dual commitments, you can cultivate success in both your professional realms and set the stage for achieving your entrepreneurial aspirations.

- Effective Time Blocking Techniques

Time blocking is a powerful time management technique that involves scheduling specific blocks of time for different tasks or activities. This comprehensive discussion explores various effective time-blocking techniques to help you maximize productivity, maintain focus, and achieve your goals.

1. **Prioritize and Identify Key Tasks:**

Begin by identifying and prioritizing key tasks that align with your goals. Categorize tasks based on urgency and importance. This foundational step sets the stage for effective time blocking, ensuring that your allocated time addresses high-impact activities.

2. **Daily, Weekly, and Monthly Planning:**

Implement a structured planning approach. Daily planning helps you allocate time for immediate tasks, while weekly and monthly planning allows for a broader perspective. This layered approach ensures that short-term objectives align with long-term goals, fostering strategic time management.

3. **Time Blocking for Focus Periods:**

Allocate focused time blocks for specific types of work. For example, designate a block for creative tasks, another for routine administrative work, and a separate block for meetings or collaboration. This minimizes task-switching and enhances concentration within each dedicated period.

4. The Pomodoro Technique:

Embrace the Pomodoro Technique, which involves working in short, focused bursts (typically 25 minutes) followed by a brief break. Each work period is a dedicated time block, promoting sustained attention and preventing burnout. After four cycles, take a more extended break.

5. Theme Days or Weeks:

Organize your schedule around themed days or weeks, where specific types of tasks dominate each period. For instance, designate Mondays for strategic planning, Tuesdays for client meetings, and Wednesdays for creative projects. Theming enhances efficiency and reduces the mental load.

6. Time Blocking for Personal Activities:

Extend time blocking to personal activities, ensuring a balanced schedule. Allocate time for exercise, family, and relaxation. Integrating personal time blocks enhances overall well-being and prevents professional burnout.

7. Buffer Time Between Blocks:

Incorporate buffer time between time blocks to accommodate unexpected delays or transitions between tasks. Buffer time provides flexibility, reduces stress, and prevents the ripple effect of one delayed task affecting the next.

8. Batching Similar Tasks:

Group similar tasks together in a single time block. Batching reduces the cognitive load associated with task-switching, as your mind can stay focused on a specific type of work. This technique is particularly effective for routine or repetitive tasks.

9. Time Blocking for Learning and Development:

Dedicate time blocks for continuous learning and skill development. Whether it's reading industry articles, taking online courses, or attending webinars, allocating time for professional growth ensures you stay ahead in your field.

10. Digital Detox Time Blocks:

Introduce time blocks for digital detox, where you disconnect from emails, social media, and other digital distractions. This dedicated time fosters deep work, creativity, and mental rejuvenation.

11. Adaptability and Flexibility:

Maintain flexibility within your time-blocking system. Recognize that unexpected priorities may arise, and be willing to adjust your schedule accordingly. An adaptable approach ensures your time-blocking system remains practical and sustainable.

12. Reflect and Iterate:

Regularly reflect on the effectiveness of your time-blocking strategy. Assess whether your allocated time aligns with your actual workflow and adjust your approach accordingly. Continuous reflection and iteration are integral to optimizing your time management system.

13. **Utilize Time Management Tools:**

Leverage time management tools and apps to enhance your time-blocking technique. Calendar apps, task management tools, and productivity apps can streamline the planning and execution of your time blocks.

14. **Communication and Collaboration Blocks:**

Allocate specific time blocks for communication and collaboration. This could include responding to emails, participating in team meetings, or engaging with clients. Segregating communication prevents constant interruptions throughout the day.

15. **Experiment with Different Structures:**

Experiment with different time block structures to find what works best for you. Whether it's shorter, more frequent blocks or longer, intensive sessions, tailor your approach to match your personal preferences and energy levels.

16. **Delegate and Outsource Blocks:**

Designate time blocks for delegation and outsourcing tasks that others can handle. This not only frees up your time for high-priority activities but also leverages the skills of your team or external support.

By incorporating these effective time-blocking techniques into your routine, you can harness the power of focused, intentional work. Time blocking not only enhances productivity but also provides a structured framework for balancing various responsibilities and achieving both short-term and long-term goals.

- Prioritizing Tasks for Maximum Impact

Effectively prioritizing tasks is a fundamental skill for achieving maximum impact in your personal and professional endeavors. This comprehensive discussion explores a strategic process to prioritize tasks, ensuring that your time and energy are directed towards high-impact activities that align with your goals.

1. Define Clear Goals and Objectives:

Begin by establishing clear goals and objectives. Understand your overarching mission and the specific outcomes you aim to achieve. Clearly defined goals provide a framework for prioritization, allowing you to align tasks with your broader aspirations.

2. Categorize Tasks Based on Importance and Urgency:

Use the Eisenhower Matrix or a similar framework to categorize tasks based on their importance and urgency. Tasks can be classified into four quadrants: important and urgent, important but not urgent, urgent but not important, and neither urgent nor important. This categorization guides your prioritization strategy.

3. Identify High-Impact Activities:

Identify tasks that contribute significantly to your goals. These high-impact activities may not always be urgent but are crucial for long-term success. Prioritizing these tasks ensures that your efforts align with the most meaningful and impactful aspects of your work.

4. Consider Time Constraints and Deadlines:

Take into account time constraints and deadlines associated with tasks. Prioritize activities that have imminent deadlines or are time-sensitive. However, avoid falling into the trap of prioritizing solely based on urgency, as this may neglect important but less time-sensitive tasks.

5. Evaluate Resources and Dependencies:

Consider the resources required for each task and any dependencies between tasks. Tasks that rely on external factors or are resource-intensive may need early prioritization. This assessment ensures that you can manage your resources efficiently.

6. Assess Impact on Long-Term Goals:

Evaluate how each task contributes to your long-term goals. Prioritize tasks that align with your strategic objectives and vision. This forward-thinking approach prevents getting caught up in the urgency of the moment at the expense of your broader aspirations.

7. Use the 2-Minute Rule:

Adopt the 2-Minute Rule introduced by productivity expert David Allen. If a task takes less than two minutes to complete, do it immediately. This rule eliminates small, quick tasks from cluttering your to-do list and allows you to maintain momentum.

8. Apply the Pareto Principle (80/20 Rule):

Leverage the Pareto Principle, which states that roughly 80% of the effects come from 20% of the causes. Identify and prioritize the tasks that fall within this vital 20%, as they are likely to have a disproportionate impact on your overall outcomes.

9. Rank Tasks Using a Scoring System:

Develop a scoring system to rank tasks based on criteria such as importance, alignment with goals, and potential impact. Assign numerical values to each criterion and use the cumulative score to prioritize tasks. This systematic approach adds objectivity to your prioritization process.

10. Focus on One Task at a Time:

Embrace the power of single-tasking. While multitasking may seem efficient, focusing on one task at a time allows for deeper concentration and higher-quality output. Prioritize tasks sequentially, giving your full attention to each before moving on to the next.

11. Regularly Review and Adjust Priorities:

Conduct regular reviews of your task list and priorities. As circumstances change, be willing to adjust your priorities accordingly. A dynamic approach to prioritization ensures that your efforts remain aligned with evolving goals and external factors.

12. Delegate Non-Core Activities:

Identify tasks that are not aligned with your core competencies or high-impact activities and consider delegating them. Delegation allows you to focus on tasks that truly require your unique skills and expertise, optimizing your overall effectiveness.

13. Create a Daily Task List:

Develop a daily task list that outlines the prioritized activities for the day. Having a clear agenda helps you maintain focus and guides your work throughout the day. Regularly reassess and adjust the daily list as needed.

14. Utilize Technology and Tools:

Leverage productivity tools and technology to aid in prioritization. Project management apps, task organizers, and digital calendars can streamline the process, providing visibility into tasks, deadlines, and progress.

15. Seek Input and Collaboration:

Consult with colleagues, mentors, or team members when determining task priorities. Collaborative decision-making can provide diverse perspectives and ensure that collective priorities align with overarching goals.

16. Balance Short-Term and Long-Term Priorities:

Maintain a balance between short-term and long-term priorities. While addressing immediate needs is essential, consistently prioritizing tasks that contribute to your long-term success prevents the neglect of strategic objectives.

17. Practice Mindfulness and Reflection:

Cultivate mindfulness in your work and regularly reflect on your priorities. Being present in the moment allows you to make intentional decisions about where to direct your efforts. Reflective practices enhance self-awareness and improve decision-making.

By systematically applying these prioritization strategies, you can streamline your workflow, increase your productivity, and ensure that your efforts are consistently directed toward tasks that make a substantial impact. Prioritizing tasks strategically not only optimizes your time but also propels you closer to achieving your overarching goals and aspirations.

- Overcoming Procrastination and Burnout

Procrastination and burnout are formidable challenges that can impede personal and professional growth. This comprehensive discussion delves into a strategic and holistic process to overcome these obstacles, fostering sustained productivity and well-being.

Understanding Procrastination:

1. Identify Root Causes:

Begin by identifying the root causes of procrastination. Whether it stems from fear of failure, lack of motivation, or overwhelming tasks, understanding the underlying factors is crucial for developing targeted solutions.

2.   Tackle large tasks by breaking them down into smaller, more manageable components. This not only makes the work less daunting but also provides a sense of accomplishment as each subtask is completed.

3. Set Realistic Goals:

Establish realistic and achievable goals. Unrealistic expectations can lead to procrastination due to a perceived inability to meet the demands. Setting achievable milestones fosters a sense of progress and reduces the likelihood of procrastination.

4. Utilize the Two-Minute Rule:

Implement the Two-Minute Rule, introduced by productivity expert David Allen. If a task takes less than two minutes to complete, do it immediately. This small but impactful rule prevents the accumulation of minor tasks that can contribute to procrastination.

5. Create a Structured Routine:

Develop a structured daily routine. Consistent routines create a sense of stability, making it easier to transition into work mode. Include dedicated time blocks for specific tasks, reducing the temptation to procrastinate.

6. Leverage the Pomodoro Technique:

Embrace the Pomodoro Technique, which involves working in focused intervals (typically 25 minutes) followed by short breaks. Breaking the work into manageable segments prevents burnout and helps maintain sustained focus.

7. Cultivate Intrinsic Motivation:

Cultivate intrinsic motivation by connecting tasks to your values and long-term goals. Understanding the purpose behind your work enhances engagement and diminishes the likelihood of procrastination.

8. Eliminate Distractions:

Identify and eliminate distractions in your environment. Create a dedicated workspace, turn off non-essential notifications, and establish boundaries to minimize interruptions. A focused environment is conducive to overcoming procrastination.

Addressing Burnout:

1. Recognize Early Warning Signs:

Be vigilant for early warning signs of burnout, such as fatigue, lack of motivation, or declining performance. Recognizing these signals allows for proactive intervention before burnout intensifies.

2. Prioritize Self-Care:

Prioritize self-care as a non-negotiable aspect of your routine. Ensure sufficient sleep, engage in regular exercise, and allocate time for activities that bring joy and relaxation. Self-care is a powerful preventive measure against burnout.

3. Set Realistic Work Boundaries:

Establish clear boundaries between work and personal life. Define specific work hours and resist the temptation to consistently work beyond them. Setting realistic boundaries prevents work-related stress from permeating your personal life.

4. Learn to Delegate:

Develop the ability to delegate tasks. Understand that not every responsibility needs to rest on your shoulders. Delegating tasks not only reduces your workload but also provides growth opportunities for others.

5. **Regular Breaks and Time Off:**

Integrate regular breaks into your workday, allowing moments for relaxation and rejuvenation. Additionally, take periodic vacations or extended breaks to recharge. Time away from work is essential for preventing burnout.

6. **Seek Support and Communication:**

Foster open communication with colleagues, friends, or family about your workload and feelings of burnout. Seeking support and sharing your challenges creates a network that can offer insights and assistance.

7. **Establish Achievable Goals:**

Set achievable and realistic goals. Constantly pursuing unattainable objectives contributes to burnout. Establish milestones that are challenging yet feasible, promoting a sense of accomplishment without excessive stress.

8. **Rotate Tasks and Projects:**

Rotate between different tasks and projects to introduce variety into your routine. Monotony can contribute to burnout, and diversifying your responsibilities helps maintain interest and enthusiasm.

9. Continuous Learning and Growth:

Prioritize continuous learning and professional growth. Engaging in activities that expand your skills and knowledge fosters a sense of purpose and prevents stagnation, mitigating the risk of burnout.

10. Mindfulness and Stress Reduction Techniques:

Practice mindfulness and stress reduction techniques, such as meditation or deep breathing exercises. These practices promote mental well-being, reduce stress levels, and enhance resilience against burnout.

11. Regularly Assess Workload:

Regularly assess your workload and commitments. Be realistic about your capacity and avoid overcommitting. Regular self-assessment helps identify potential sources of burnout before they become overwhelming.

12. **Establish a Support System:**

Cultivate a support system within your workplace and personal life. Surround yourself with individuals who understand the challenges you face and provide encouragement. A supportive network can offer valuable perspectives and assistance.

13. **Professional Development and Skill Enhancement:**

Invest in professional development and skill enhancement. Acquiring new skills and taking on challenges aligned with your interests can invigorate your work, reducing the likelihood of burnout.

14. **Regularly Reassess Goals and Values:**

Periodically reassess your professional and personal goals and values. Ensure that your current pursuits align with your intrinsic motivations and long-term aspirations. Adjustments to align with evolving priorities can prevent burnout.

15. **Consider Seeking Professional Help:**

If feelings of burnout persist, consider seeking professional help from a counsellor or therapist. Professional support provides a confidential space to address underlying issues and develop coping strategies.

By adopting a holistic approach that addresses the root causes of procrastination and burnout, you can cultivate sustained productivity and well-being. Combining proactive strategies, self-awareness, and intentional self-care creates a resilient foundation for navigating the challenges of work and life.

CHAPTER 5: MARKETING AND GROWING YOUR SIDE HUSTLE

Welcome to the dynamic realm of "Marketing and Growing Your Side Hustle," a chapter dedicated to unravelling the strategies and tactics essential for propelling your side hustle into a flourishing venture. In the ever-evolving digital landscape, effective marketing is the catalyst that transforms passion into profitability, and strategic growth becomes the linchpin for long-term success.

Navigating the Digital Landscape:

In an era where connectivity and visibility are paramount, mastering the art of marketing is not just a choice but a necessity for any aspiring entrepreneur. This chapter serves as your compass through the intricacies of digital marketing, providing insights and actionable steps to not only promote your side hustle but also to foster sustainable growth.

Key Themes Explored in this Chapter:

1. Crafting a Compelling Brand Story:

Uncover the power of storytelling in marketing. Learn how to articulate a compelling brand story that resonates with your audience, instils trust, and sets the foundation for effective marketing communications.

2. Strategic Online Presence:

Dive into the strategies for establishing and optimizing your online presence. From creating a user-friendly website to leveraging social media platforms, explore avenues that enhance visibility, engage your audience, and elevate your brand.

3. Content Marketing and SEO Strategies:

Delve into the world of content marketing and search engine optimization (SEO). Understand how creating valuable content not only establishes your expertise but also boosts your online discoverability, driving organic growth.

4. Social Media Mastery:

Unpack the intricacies of social media marketing. From choosing the right platforms to crafting engaging content, discover how to harness the immense potential of social media for brand promotion, audience engagement, and community building.

5. Email Marketing Excellence:

Explore the effectiveness of email marketing as a powerful tool for nurturing relationships with your audience. Learn how to build and maintain an email list, create compelling campaigns, and drive conversions through targeted communication.

6. Paid Advertising Strategies:

Navigate the landscape of paid advertising, including pay-per-click (PPC) campaigns and social media ads. Understand how to strategically invest in paid promotions to amplify your reach and drive targeted traffic to your side hustle.

7. Analytics and Data-Driven Decision-Making:

Embrace the role of analytics in refining your marketing strategies. Discover how data-driven insights can guide your decision-making process, allowing you to optimize campaigns, understand audience behavior, and adapt to market trends.

8. Influencer Collaborations and Partnerships:

Uncover the potential of influencer marketing and collaborations. Explore how partnerships with influencers and other businesses can amplify your reach, enhance credibility, and open doors to new opportunities.

9. Customer Relationship Management (CRM):

Implement effective customer relationship management strategies. Understand the importance of building strong relationships with your customers, fostering loyalty, and leveraging satisfied customers as brand advocates.

10. **Scaling for Growth:**

Learn the art of scaling your side hustle for sustained growth. From expanding product offerings to entering new markets, explore strategies that position your venture for long-term success in a competitive landscape.

The Intersection of Creativity and Strategy:

This chapter serves as a dynamic intersection where creativity meets strategy, empowering you to navigate the complexities of marketing and growth with finesse. Whether you're a seasoned entrepreneur or embarking on your first side hustle, the insights within these pages are designed to equip you with the knowledge and tools needed to thrive in the competitive digital marketplace.

Prepare to embark on a journey that goes beyond traditional marketing paradigms. The strategies and principles presented here are not just about promoting your side hustle; they are about cultivating a brand, building a community, and fostering a trajectory of growth that aligns with your unique entrepreneurial vision. Let the exploration of "Marketing and Growing Your Side Hustle" be the catalyst for transforming your passion into a thriving and impactful venture.

- Crafting a Compelling Brand Story

Crafting a compelling brand story is more than narrating the journey of your side hustle; it's about creating an emotional connection with your audience, instilling trust, and differentiating your brand in a crowded marketplace. In this comprehensive discussion, we delve into the strategic process of shaping a narrative that resonates, captivates, and leaves a lasting imprint on the minds of your audience.

1. **Define Your Brand Identity:**

   Begin by defining the core identity of your brand. What values, principles, and beliefs underpin your side hustle? Clearly articulate the mission and vision that drive your venture, providing a solid foundation for your brand story.

2. Understand Your Audience:

Before penning your story, intimately understand your target audience. What are their needs, desires, and pain points? Tailoring your narrative to resonate with your audience's emotions and aspirations establishes a powerful connection.

3. Identify Your Unique Selling Proposition (USP):

Uncover the unique aspects that set your side hustle apart. Whether it's a distinctive product feature, a novel approach, or a compelling mission, identifying your Unique Selling Proposition provides a focal point for your brand story.

4. Craft a Compelling Origin Tale:

Every brand has an origin story waiting to be told. Share the journey that led to the creation of your side hustle, highlighting the challenges overcome and the passion that fuels your endeavors. An authentic origin story humanizes your brand, making it relatable and engaging.

5. Weave Emotion into Your Narrative:

Emotion is the secret sauce of a compelling brand story. Infuse your narrative with emotions that resonate—whether it's joy, empathy, or inspiration. Emotional connections create memorable experiences that linger in the minds of your audience.

6. Characterize Your Brand as a Hero:

Position your brand as a hero in the story. Outline the challenges (or "villains") your audience faces, and illustrate how your side hustle, as the hero, provides solutions and leads them toward success. This hero's journey narrative instils confidence and trust.

7. Maintain Consistency Across Platforms:

Consistency is key in brand storytelling. Ensure that your narrative remains coherent across all platforms—your website, social media, and marketing materials. A unified story builds a cohesive brand identity and reinforces your messaging.

8. Use Visuals to Enhance the Story:

Complement your narrative with visuals that reinforce the brand story. Whether through logo design, imagery, or graphics, visuals create a visual language that enhances the emotional impact of your storytelling.

9. Engage in Interactive Storytelling:

Encourage audience participation through interactive storytelling. Whether through social media polls, user-generated content, or storytelling campaigns, invite your audience to be part of the narrative. Interactive elements enhance engagement and create a sense of community.

10. Highlight Customer Success Stories:

Showcase real-life customer success stories as integral chapters in your brand narrative. Customer testimonials and case studies serve as proof points for the efficacy of your products or services, fostering credibility and trust.

11. Embrace Transparency and Authenticity:

Transparency builds trust. Be open and authentic in sharing your brand story, including both successes and challenges. Authenticity resonates with consumers, fostering a sense of transparency that strengthens the bond between your brand and audience.

12. Adapt Your Story as Your Brand Evolves:

Brands evolve, and so should their stories. Regularly reassess and adapt your brand story to reflect changes in your business, market trends, or societal shifts. An evolving narrative ensures that your brand remains relevant and resonant.

13. Integrate Brand Storytelling in Marketing Campaigns:

Infuse your marketing campaigns with elements of your brand story. Whether through advertisements, social media campaigns, or product launches, align your marketing efforts with the overarching narrative to reinforce your brand identity.

14. Seek Feedback and Iterate:

Solicit feedback from your audience to gauge the impact of your brand story. Analyze responses, monitor engagement metrics, and iterate based on insights. Continuous refinement ensures that your brand story remains dynamic and effective.

15. Educate and Inspire Through Your Narrative:

Beyond selling a product or service, use your brand story to educate and inspire. Position your side hustle as a source of knowledge, empowerment, or inspiration. An educational narrative fosters a sense of value beyond transactions.

Crafting a compelling brand story is an ongoing process that requires finesse, empathy, and an understanding of the ever-changing landscape of your audience. As you embark on this journey of storytelling, envision your brand not just as a product or service but as a narrative that resonates with the hearts and minds of your audience, building a community that champions your unique story in the broader marketplace.

- Leveraging Social Media Platforms

In today's interconnected world, social media platforms are integral to brand visibility, audience engagement, and business growth. This comprehensive discussion outlines the strategic process of leveraging social media to amplify your side hustle, foster meaningful connections, and cultivate a dynamic online presence.

1. **Define Your Social Media Objectives:**

Begin by defining clear objectives for your social media efforts. Whether it's increasing brand awareness, driving website traffic, or boosting sales, establishing specific and measurable goals provides a roadmap for your social media strategy.

2. Identify Your Target Audience:

Understand your target audience—their demographics, preferences, and behaviors. Tailoring your content to resonate with your audience creates a more impactful and personalized social media experience, fostering engagement and loyalty.

3. Choose the Right Platforms:

Select social media platforms that align with your target audience and business goals. Different platforms cater to diverse demographics and content formats. Consider factors such as user demographics, content type, and engagement patterns when choosing where to establish your social media presence.

4. Optimize Your Profiles:

Create compelling and consistent profiles across chosen platforms. Utilize high-quality visuals, and concise and engaging descriptions, and incorporate relevant keywords. An optimized profile establishes a strong first impression and encourages users to explore your content.

5. Develop a Content Strategy:

Craft a robust content strategy that aligns with your brand voice and resonates with your audience. Include a mix of content types, such as informative posts, engaging visuals, videos, and user-generated content. A diverse content strategy keeps your feed dynamic and interesting.

6. Establish a Posting Schedule:

Consistency is key in social media. Develop a posting schedule that aligns with the habits of your target audience. Whether daily, weekly, or bi-weekly, a consistent posting schedule helps maintain visibility and engagement.

7. Engage with Your Audience:

Actively engage with your audience through comments, direct messages, and discussions.

Respond promptly, express gratitude, and participate in conversations related to your industry. Authentic engagement fosters a sense of community and builds trust.

8. Utilize Visual Storytelling:

Leverage the power of visual storytelling. Humans are inherently drawn to visuals, so incorporate eye-catching images, infographics, and videos into your content. Visuals convey messages quickly and enhance the overall appeal of your brand.

9. Leverage Hashtags Strategically:

Implement hashtags strategically to increase discoverability. Research and use relevant hashtags in your posts to tap into larger conversations within your industry or niche. Create a branded hashtag to encourage user-generated content and community engagement.

10. Run Targeted Advertising Campaigns:

Invest in targeted advertising campaigns on social media platforms. Utilize the platforms' advertising tools to create highly targeted campaigns based on demographics, interests, and behaviors. Paid advertising can amplify your reach and drive specific outcomes.

11. **Monitor Analytics and Insights:**

Regularly analyze social media analytics and insights. Evaluate metrics such as engagement rates, reach, and conversion rates. These insights provide valuable data for refining your strategy, understanding audience behavior, and optimizing future content.

12. **Collaborate with Influencers:**

Explore influencer collaborations to expand your reach. Identify influencers within your niche or industry whose audience aligns with your target demographic. Collaborations introduce your brand to new audiences and lend credibility through trusted influencers.

13. **Host Contests and Giveaways:**

Engage your audience through contests and giveaways. Encourage participation by asking users to share, tag friends, or follow your page. Contests generate excitement, increase visibility, and create a sense of community around your brand.

14. **Stay Informed About Trends:**

Stay abreast of social media trends and platform updates. Social media evolves rapidly, and staying informed allows you to adapt your strategy, leverage new features, and capitalize on emerging trends to remain relevant in the digital landscape.

15. **Crisis Management and Reputation Building:**

Develop a crisis management plan for handling potential issues. Address negative feedback promptly and professionally, demonstrating a commitment to customer satisfaction. Proactively build and maintain a positive online reputation through transparent communication and exceptional customer service.

16. **Measure ROI and Adjust Strategies:**

Assess the return on investment (ROI) of your social media efforts. Track key performance indicators (KPIs) related to your objectives and adjust your strategies accordingly. Data-driven decision-making ensures that your social media efforts align with business goals.

Leveraging social media platforms effectively requires a combination of strategic planning, engaging content, and active community management. By aligning your social media strategy with your overall business objectives and consistently adapting to the dynamic nature of online platforms, you can harness the full potential of social media to propel your side hustle toward sustainable growth and success.

- Implementing Effective Marketing Strategies

Implementing effective marketing strategies is essential for propelling your side hustle to new heights of success. This comprehensive discussion outlines a strategic and holistic process to create, execute, and refine marketing strategies that align with your business goals, resonate with your target audience, and foster sustainable growth.

1. **Conduct a Comprehensive Market Analysis:**

Begin by conducting a thorough analysis of the market in which your side hustle operates. Understand industry trends, competitor landscape, and the needs and preferences of your target audience. This foundational step informs the development of strategies that stand out in the marketplace.

2. Define Clear Marketing Objectives:

Clearly define your marketing objectives. Whether it's increasing brand awareness, driving sales, expanding market share, or launching a new product, having specific and measurable objectives provides direction for your marketing efforts.

3. Identify Your Target Audience:

Precisely identify and understand your target audience. Develop detailed buyer personas to guide your marketing strategies. Knowing the demographics, behaviors, and preferences of your audience allows for more personalized and effective campaigns.

4. Craft a Unique Value Proposition:

Articulate a compelling and unique value proposition that sets your side hustle apart from competitors. Communicate what makes your products or services special and how they address the specific needs of your target audience.

5. Select the Right Marketing Channels:

Choose marketing channels that align with your objectives and target audience. Whether it's social media, email marketing, content marketing, paid advertising, or a combination of these, selecting the right channels ensures that your message reaches the right audience.

6. Develop a Content Marketing Strategy:

Craft a robust content marketing strategy. Create valuable and relevant content that educates, entertains, and engages your audience. From blog posts and videos to infographics and social media updates, diverse and high-quality content enhances your brand's online presence.

7. Implement Search Engine Optimization (SEO):

Integrate SEO strategies to enhance your online visibility. Optimize your website and content to rank higher in search engine results. A strong SEO foundation ensures that your side hustle is easily discoverable by potential customers.

8. Utilize Email Marketing Effectively:

Implement email marketing campaigns to nurture relationships with your audience. Develop targeted and personalized email campaigns that provide value, drive engagement, and guide leads through the sales funnel.

9. Engage in Social Media Marketing:

Leverage the power of social media to connect with your audience. Develop a social media strategy that aligns with your brand voice, engages followers, and promotes community building. Consistent and authentic social media presence enhances brand visibility.

10. Incorporate Paid Advertising Campaigns:

Invest in paid advertising campaigns strategically. Utilize platforms like Google Ads, Facebook Ads, or other relevant channels to reach a wider audience. Paid advertising can accelerate brand exposure and drive targeted traffic.

11. Harness Influencer Marketing:

Explore influencer marketing collaborations. Partner with influencers in your industry or niche to expand your reach and tap into their engaged audience. Authentic influencer partnerships can build credibility and trust.

12. Implement Data Analytics and Measurement:

Integrate data analytics tools to measure the performance of your marketing strategies. Track key performance indicators (KPIs), analyze consumer behavior, and gather insights to refine and optimize your future campaigns.

13. Utilize Customer Relationship Management (CRM) Systems:

Implement CRM systems to manage and analyze customer interactions. CRM tools help in understanding customer preferences, streamlining communication, and fostering long-term relationships. A customer-centric approach enhances retention and loyalty.

14. Optimize for Mobile Devices:

Ensure that your marketing strategies are optimized for mobile devices. With a growing number of users accessing content on smartphones and tablets, mobile optimization is critical for reaching and engaging a broad audience.

15. Seek Customer Feedback and Iterate:

Actively seek feedback from your customers. Use surveys, reviews, and social media interactions to gather insights into customer satisfaction and preferences. Apply this feedback to iterate and enhance your marketing strategies continuously.

16. Stay Agile and Adapt to Trends:

Remain agile in the dynamic landscape of marketing. Stay informed about emerging trends, new technologies, and shifts in consumer behavior. The ability to adapt to changing circumstances ensures the relevance and effectiveness of your marketing strategies.

17. **Build a Consistent Brand Image:**

Maintain a consistent brand image across all marketing channels. Consistency in messaging, visuals, and tone creates a cohesive and memorable brand identity. A unified brand image contributes to brand recognition and trust.

18. **Balance Short-Term and Long-Term Strategies:**

Strike a balance between short-term and long-term marketing strategies. While short-term tactics may drive immediate results, long-term strategies contribute to sustained growth and brand building. Develop a holistic marketing plan that addresses both aspects.

19. Compliance with Legal and Ethical Standards:

Ensure that your marketing strategies comply with legal and ethical standards. Transparency, honesty, and adherence to regulations build trust with your audience and protect your brand reputation.

20. Celebrate and Showcase Successes:

Celebrate milestones and successes in your marketing efforts. Share success stories, customer testimonials, and achievements with your audience. Celebrating successes creates positive brand associations and reinforces your brand narrative.

Implementing effective marketing strategies is an ongoing and iterative process that requires a deep understanding of your business, target audience, and the broader market landscape. By adopting a strategic and customer-centric approach, continually analyzing performance, and adapting to evolving trends, you can cultivate a resilient and impactful marketing strategy that propels your side hustle toward sustainable growth and success.

- Scaling Your Side Hustle for Long-Term Success

Scaling your side hustle involves planning, resource management, and strategic decision-making to propel your venture toward sustained success. This comprehensive discussion outlines a systematic process to scale your side hustle, taking into account factors such as market dynamics, operational efficiency, and customer satisfaction.

1. **Evaluate Current Business Operations:**

Begin by conducting a thorough evaluation of your current business operations. Assess the efficiency of your processes, identify bottlenecks, and determine areas that require optimization. A clear understanding of your existing operations is foundational for effective scaling.

2. Define Clear Business Objectives:

Clearly define your business objectives for scaling. Whether it's expanding market reach, increasing revenue, or launching new products/services, well-defined objectives provide direction and purpose for your scaling efforts.

3. Identify Scalable Revenue Streams:

Explore and identify scalable revenue streams within your side hustle. Assess products or services with high profit margins, potential for repeat business, or opportunities for upselling. Focusing on scalable revenue streams contributes to sustainable growth.

4. Build a Scalable Infrastructure:

Develop a scalable infrastructure that can accommodate increased demand. This includes optimizing technology systems, streamlining processes, and ensuring that your business can handle growth without compromising quality or efficiency.

5. Invest in Technology and Automation:

Leverage technology and automation to enhance operational efficiency. Implement tools and systems that automate repetitive tasks, streamline workflows, and improve overall productivity. Technology investments contribute to scalability by reducing manual workload.

6. Expand Your Customer Base:

Identify strategies to expand your customer base. This may involve targeting new demographics, entering new markets, or implementing customer acquisition campaigns. Expanding your customer base diversifies your revenue streams and increases market share.

7. Enhance Marketing and Branding:

Invest in marketing and branding efforts to enhance visibility and awareness. Utilize strategic marketing campaigns, social media strategies, and influencer collaborations to amplify your brand presence. Effective marketing contributes to attracting new customers and retaining existing ones.

8. Optimize Customer Retention Strategies:

Implement robust customer retention strategies to ensure long-term success. This may include loyalty programs, personalized communication, and exceptional customer service. Prioritizing customer satisfaction contributes to repeat business and positive word-of-mouth.

9. Diversify Product or Service Offerings:

Explore opportunities to diversify your product or service offerings. Introduce complementary products or expand your service portfolio to cater to evolving customer needs. Diversification contributes to increased revenue and customer engagement.

10. Explore Strategic Partnerships:

Identify and explore strategic partnerships that align with your scaling objectives. Collaborate with other businesses or influencers to expand your reach, tap into new markets, and leverage shared resources. Strategic partnerships can accelerate your growth trajectory.

11. Evaluate Financial Health and Funding Options:

Assess the financial health of your side hustle and explore funding options for scaling. This may involve reinvesting profits, seeking external investment, or exploring loans. Adequate financial planning ensures that your scaling efforts are supported by a sustainable financial foundation.

12. Develop a Scalable Team:

Build a scalable team capable of handling increased responsibilities. Assess staffing needs, hire strategically, and invest in employee development. A skilled and adaptable team is crucial for scaling your side hustle without compromising on quality.

13. Implement Efficient Inventory Management:

If applicable, optimize your inventory management processes. Efficient inventory management prevents stockouts, reduces holding costs, and ensures that you can meet increased demand without excess inventory. This is particularly important for product-based side hustles.

14. Adopt Agile Decision-Making:

Cultivate an agile decision-making process that allows for quick adjustments to changing circumstances. Embrace flexibility and adaptability in your approach to scaling, allowing you to respond proactively to market shifts and emerging opportunities.

15. **Measure and Analyze Key Performance Indicators (KPIs):**

Implement a robust system for measuring and analyzing key performance indicators (KPIs). Regularly assess metrics such as revenue growth, customer acquisition costs, and customer lifetime value. Data-driven insights guide your scaling strategies and enable informed decision-making.

16. **Maintain a Customer-Centric Approach:**

Retain a customer-centric focus throughout the scaling process. Listen to customer feedback, address concerns promptly, and adapt your offerings based on customer preferences. Prioritizing the customer experience contributes to long-term success.

17. **Plan for Scalability in Marketing and Sales:**

Design marketing and sales strategies with scalability in mind. Ensure that your marketing campaigns can accommodate increased demand and that your sales processes can efficiently handle a growing customer base.

18. Regularly Review and Iterate Strategies:

Conduct regular reviews of your scaling strategies. Evaluate the effectiveness of implemented initiatives, identify areas for improvement, and iteratively refine your scaling plan based on performance data and market feedback.

19. Prepare for Potential Challenges:

Anticipate potential challenges associated with scaling, such as increased competition, supply chain disruptions, or shifts in consumer behavior. Develop contingency plans to address challenges and ensure resilience in the face of unforeseen obstacles.

20. Celebrate Milestones and Successes:

Celebrate achievements and milestones as you scale your side hustle. Acknowledge the hard work of your team, recognize significant accomplishments, and use positive reinforcement to maintain

Motivation and morale.

Scaling your side hustle is a dynamic and multifaceted process that requires a strategic mindset, adaptability, and a commitment to continuous improvement. By systematically addressing key components such as infrastructure, customer engagement, and financial planning, you can navigate the complexities of scaling and position your side hustle for sustainable long-term success.

CONCLUSION

As we reach the culmination of "The Successful Side Hustle: How to Make Money Outside of Your Day Job," I extend my heartfelt gratitude for joining me on this transformative exploration of entrepreneurial endeavors. Throughout the chapters, we've navigated the intricate landscapes of ideation, passion discovery, strategic planning, and effective execution, unveiling the secrets to crafting a thriving side hustle.

This journey has been more than a guide; it's been an invitation to embrace the limitless possibilities that lie beyond the confines of a traditional nine-to-five. It is a celebration of the diverse passions, talents, and aspirations that reside within each of us, waiting to be harnessed and translated into tangible success.

As you reflect on the insights shared within these pages, I encourage you to see your side hustle not just as a means to supplement your income but as a dynamic force capable of reshaping your financial landscape and personal fulfillment. The lessons learned—from recognizing the importance of side hustles in the evolving economy to mastering the delicate balance between passion and profitability— are the building blocks of your entrepreneurial journey.

Remember, your side hustle is not defined solely by financial gains but by the impact it has on your life, the lives of others, and the broader community. It's a testament to your creativity, resilience, and unwavering commitment to realizing your dreams.

As you embark on the exciting road ahead, let this conclusion be a catalyst for sustained motivation. Embrace the challenges as opportunities for growth, view setbacks as lessons in resilience, and relish every success as a testament to your dedication. Continue to refine your strategies, adapt to the evolving landscape, and revel in the joy of pursuing endeavors that align with your passions.

May your side hustle journey be marked by innovation, fulfillment, and the unwavering belief that success is not just a destination but a dynamic and evolving process? With the tools and insights acquired within these pages, you have the foundation to turn your side hustle into a force of positive change—both in your life and in the broader entrepreneurial ecosystem.

Thank you for entrusting me as your guide on this journey. Your commitment to crafting a successful side hustle is a testament to your vision and resilience. As you close this book, may it serve as a source of inspiration and a reference guide for the exciting chapters that await you in the world of successful side hustles.

Here's to the flourishing ventures, impactful contributions, and boundless possibilities that lie ahead. May your side hustle not only thrive but also bring you a profound sense of fulfillment, purpose, and lasting success.